Character

by

Design

Bontiveron Leonard, MBA

Introduction

This book is a biblical perspective about Character. Your Character has been designed by God, in His Word. He has already given you the ability to develop your Character. Developing good Character, in all aspects of your life, glorifies God.

The moral fiber of our world is decaying. "Righteousness [moral and spiritual integrity and virtuous Character] exalts a nation, but sin is a disgrace to any people." (Proverbs 14:34)

We must return back to God. We have become prodigal sons and daughters of the Most High God. The more we move away from the Truth of the Glorious Gospel, the more darkness increases over our lives and on earth.

"The eye is the lamp of the body. So if your eye is clear [spiritually perceptive], your whole body will be full of light [benefiting from God's precepts]. But if your eye is bad [spiritually blind], your whole body will be full of darkness [devoid of God's precepts]. So if the [very] light inside you [your inner self, your heart, your conscience] is darkness, how great and terrible is that darkness!" (Matthew 6:22-23)

"Return to Me, saith the Lord"

"Seek the Lord while He may be found; Call on Him [for salvation] while He is near. Let the wicked leave [behind] his way and the unrighteous man his thoughts; and let him return to the Lord, and He will have compassion [mercy] on him, and to our God, for He will abundantly pardon." (Isaiah 55:6-7)

Character,
not circumstance,
makes the
person.
- Booker T. Washington

Table of Contents

Chapter 1

<u>Character Defined</u>

Character is defined as:

- The aggregate of features and traits that form the individual nature of some person or thing

- Reputation

- Moral or ethical quality

- Qualities of honesty, courage, or the like; integrity; good repute

Character is universal. Principles of good Character should apply to all people from all countries and nations. Character never goes out of style. It's always fashionable to have good Character.

Character is developed with much discipline. Each of us has a unique reputation or Character that is displayed from within. Your belief system will produce Character. If your belief system is faulty, then your Character will be faulty.

Have you heard these statements said about a person?

- "What a Character"

- "What a piece of work"

These phrases usually are used to describe a negative character trait about a person.

Are you a Character?

Don't be a character – **have Character.** Life without Character is like a ship without a sail – it cannot reach its destination.

"Mark the blameless man [who is spiritually complete], and behold the upright [who walks in moral integrity], for there is a [good] future for man of peace [because a

life of honor blesses one's descendants]."
(Psalms 37:37)

We were born into a sinful world. We do not have to learn to sin. Becoming a person of Character has to be taught and developed. Your Character is a personal alignment with what you say you believe and how you act – your personal integrity. Understanding, with application, will bring change in your life. Once you understand, you can take action on it.

"For wisdom is a defense even as money is a defense, but the excellency of knowledge is that wisdom shields and preserves the life of him who has it." (Ecclesiastes 7:12)

It's wise

to have good Character!

Public and private behavior is an indication of the kind of Character you are made of. Who are you publicly? Who are you privately? *Are you the same person publicly and privately?*

"But the fruit of the Spirit [the result of His presence within us] is love [unselfish concern for others], joy, [inner] peace,

patience [not the ability to wait, but how we act while waiting], kindness, goodness, faithfulness, gentleness, self-control. Against such things there is no law."
(Galatians 5:22-23)

"The light of the righteous [within him – grows brighter and] rejoices, but the lamp of the wicked [is a temporary light and] goes out." (Proverbs 13:9)

"Better is a little with righteousness than great income [gained] with injustice."
(Proverbs 16:8)

Chapter 2

Character Developed

Our humanity consists of three parts: the Soul, the Spirit, and the Body. You are a Spirit, you have a Soul, and you live in a Body.

Character development takes place in the conscious mind inside the Soul. Within the soul abides our intellect, reasoning, and emotions. Building Character is different than learning a set of skills. Character is formed and enforced every day in the decisions we make. Character is learned and developed.

The Bible has a lot to say about being a person with Character. The Ten Commandments and The Beatitudes are examples. Our world is losing Character every minute. Christians are losing Character every day.

You can choose to develop either good or bad Character and/or to improve it. It's under your total control. You have the power to control – *you*. Only you can allow your Character to be compromised or changed.

Most people don't like change, and Character development can be painful and uncomfortable. When starting the Character building process, remember that it will take some hard work, but it's worth it. Your efforts can turn out just as you planned or better than you anticipated.

Handling success, properly tests your Character better than failure does. You are in danger of weakening your Character if your success is based solely on possessions, money, fame, or achievements.

Character is a state of being and is a matter of the heart. It is a key component of personal and professional success.

Developing and improving your Character is a lifelong process. Every time you fail to do what you know is right, your Character is compromised.

The Value of Good Character

When people hear your name, do they think of you as a person with good Character?

"A GOOD name is rather to be chosen than great riches ..." (Proverbs 22:1)

"A GOOD name is better than precious perfume ..." (Ecclesiastes 7:1)

The Character we value today will determine who we become tomorrow. Excellence in Character is essential for maintaining success.

"The hope of the righteous [those of honorable character and integrity] is joy, but the expectation of the wicked [those who oppose God and ignore His wisdom] comes to nothing." (Proverbs 10:28)

Job was a man of good Character. "There was a man in the land of Uz whose name was Job; and that man was blameless and upright, and one who feared God [with reverence] and abstained from and turned from evil [because he honored God]." (Job 1:1)

Motivations to Change

Education and knowledge can only take you so far. Fulfilling your destiny with Character brings Glory to God. Good Character is like the icing on the cake. You can get your dream job, but without Character, you will limit opportunities for promotion.

Good Character will improve your ability to achieve goals and complete difficult tasks. Your attitude is a determining factor in whether or not you will be successful. Your attitude and how you act toward other people often determines their desire to deal

with you or not, both in business and in

personal relationships.

Chapter 3

<u>Character Traits</u>

<u>Integrity</u> shows Character

"The integrity and moral courage of the upright will guide them, but the crookedness of the treacherous will destroy them." (Proverbs 11:3)

Integrity is a firm adherence to a code of especially moral values. Integrity means to be who you are. Being true to one's self, one's values, beliefs, and standards is essential when it comes to spiritual success.

"He who walks in integrity and with moral Character walks securely, but he who takes a crooked way will be discovered and punished." (Proverbs 10:9)

We must let go of the lesser, in order to obtain the greater. Old ways of thinking and bad behavior practices prevent us from manifesting the Glory of God. Be transformed by the renewing of your mind with the Word of God. (Romans 12:2)

Let the mind of Christ be in you.

"Finally, believers, whatever is true, whatever is honorable and worthy of respect, whatever is right and confirmed by God's word, whatever is pure and wholesome, whatever is lovely and brings peace, whatever is admirable and of good repute; if there is any excellence, if there is anything worthy of praise, think *continually* on these things [center your mind on them, and implant them in your heart]." (Philippians 4:8)

Allowing others to determine what we think, feel, say, and do, are pitfalls to developing good Character.

Birds of a feather flock together. There is no way you can continue to live a carnal life and also become victorious at the same time.

"Let not mercy and kindness and truth leave you [instead let these qualities define you]; Bind them [securely] around your neck, write them on the tablet of your heart." (Proverbs 3:3)

"He is a shield to those who walk in integrity [those of honorable Character and moral courage]." (Proverbs 2:7)

Trustworthiness shows Character

Being trustworthy is an admirable Character trait. People will trust a person who has a reputation of being honest, reliable, and responsible. Trust means that you will not lie, cheat, or steal, and you are true to your word.

The story of Samson and Delilah demonstrate the working of deception.

Delilah was not trustworthy, her character trait of deceit destroyed Samson.

If you are lying and/or deceiving people, you will be considered a person who is untrustworthy. God dislikes lying lips. (Proverbs 12:22)

If people trust you, they will give you more opportunities than those they do not trust. Trust can lead you to promotion and great reward.

Honesty shows Character

"A FALSE balance and dishonest business practices are extremely offensive to the Lord, but an accurate scale is His delight." (Proverbs 11:1)

A person who is considered honest is one who displays integrity, is genuine, and not deceptive or fraudulent. Honesty is characterized by truth and sincerity.

"Honesty, Character, and Integrity never change" (Zig Ziglar).

"A faithful and trustworthy witness will not lie, but a false witness speaks lies." (Proverbs 14:5)

"A FALSE witness will not go unpunished, and he who breathes out lies will not escape." (Proverbs 19:5)

Reliability shows Character

Reliability is an admirable Character trait. A reliable person is one who has a track record of doing what he or she promised to do. A reliable person does not make excuses for not being reliable. A reliable person shows up on time.

God is reliable. He is never late and always keeps His Word.

Ask yourself,

Are you reliable?

Morality shows Character

A person who upholds high standards of decent behavior can be considered as moral. A moral person is one whose conduct is good or virtuous, and they try to do what is right and ethical.

Being moral does not mean being pious and looking down on others, that is called being self-righteous. The self-righteous person is guilty of lacking Character in many areas. Doing the right thing shows Character.

"Many hardships and perplexing circumstances confront the righteous, but the Lord rescues him from them all."

(Psalm 34:19)

Is your moral compass turned on?

Loyalty shows Character

Naomi became a widow in the country of Moab. Her daughter-in-law, Ruth, was a Moabite. After Naomi's two sons died, she decided to return to her country of Bethlehem, alone.

"But Ruth said, 'Do not urge me to leave you or to turn back from following you; for where you go, I will go, and where you lodge, I will lodge. Your people will be my people, and your God, my God."
(Ruth 1:16)

Ruth was loyal to Naomi during a time when she had nothing else to gain. But the story does not end there.

"Naomi had a relative of her husband, a man of great wealth and influence, whose name was Boaz." (Ruth 2:1)

Naomi looks for a husband for Ruth to provide security and a home. She gives Ruth instructions to follow; and Boaz marries Ruth.

Courage shows Character

Deborah, a prophetess and a wife, judged over Israel. Deborah went out to war with the King, who would not go without her. So, she went out with Barak and won the war.

The victory song was, "The village ceased to be; they ceased in Israel until I, Deborah, arose; until I arose, a mother of Israel." (Judges 5:7)

Kindness shows Character

Abigail was kind, intelligent, and beautiful. (I Samuel 25:3) Nabal, her husband, was very rich; but harsh and evil in business. When King David sent messengers to greet Nabal, he turned them away. Abigail showed her kindness and wisdom when she put together a food basket and went to meet King David. The King's anger was turned away from doing Nabal any harm. When Nabal died, King David married Abigail. (I Samuel 25:39)

"Blessed [inwardly peaceful, spiritually secure, worthy of respect] are the gentle [the kind-hearted, the sweet-spirited, the self-controlled], for they will inherit the earth!" (Matthew 5:5)

Chapter 4

Character Designed

Good Character is an essential part of being a disciple of Jesus Christ. Prepare on purpose for success. You have to plan, prepare, and expect to succeed, it just doesn't happen.

You have the ability to design your Character, so use it. Nothing changes, until you change.

"In order to have something you never had, you have to do something that you never did" (Mike Murdock).

Success is coming your way.

Are you preparing?

- *Spiritually*

- *Emotionally*

- *Intellectually*

- *Physically*

How do you see yourself? What do you see yourself doing? Look inward and write the vision down?

Without a vision, you won't know how to prepare. Get a vision for your life. Without a vision, the people perish. Imagine success.

"The picture that stays inside your mind will happen in time" (Mike Murdock).

"You cannot rise above the image you have of yourself in your mind. If you want to change where you are going in life, then you have to change what you are seeing in your imagination" (Simon Bailey).

Capture your Inner Vision

"…Write the vision and engrave it plainly on [clay] tablets so that the one who passes may read it [easily and quickly] as he hastens by." (Habakkuk 2:2)

Write It.

I am doing what I was born to do and becoming who I was created to be. I have always seen myself as a public speaker. It has been my desire to write a book.

Read It. Meditate on it.

THE BIBLE SAYS...

Say It. "Death and life are in the power of the tongue." (Proverbs 18:21)

Act It. "For just as the [human] body without the spirit is dead, so faith without works [of obedience] is also dead." (James 2:26)

Receive It. "… but with God, all things are possible." (Matthew 19:26)

Believe It. "Now FAITH is the assurance [the confirmation, the title deed] of things we hope for, being the proof of things we do not see…" (Hebrews 11:1)

God has called you to be successful in life. Expand your borders and enlarge your territory.

"You cannot stay where you are and go with God" (Henry Blackaby).

Zig Ziglar said it this way:

- "You can't become what you need to be, by remaining the same."

- "You are limited by the size of your hope."

Design your Character from God's perceptive.

There is a cost to doing nothing.

It's your move.

Extremes in Good Character

Extreme personal Character traits do not necessarily enhance success but can often cause failure. It is possible to take positive Character to an extreme, like being a Miss Goody Two-Shoes. Sometimes, extreme Character traits can be a result of prideful obsession.

"Pride goes before destruction and a haughty spirit before a fall." (Proverbs 16:18)

Don't be a Poor Winner

A poor winner is a person who wins and then ridicules the loser after the victory. No one likes a poor winner. You should be modest and considerate after a victory. Modesty and consideration of the other person's feelings are an important positive trait that reveals your Character.

Chapter 5

Characteristics of God

God is the author of Character.

God is *Faithful*

I once was young and now I am older; and I have never been forsaken nor have I or my seed begged for bread.

"God is faithful [He is reliable, trustworthy and ever true to His promise – He can depended on], and through Him we were called into fellowship with His Son, Jesus Christ our Lord". (1 Corinthians 1:9)

"O Lord God of hosts, who is like You, O mighty Lord? Your faithfulness surrounds You [as an intrinsic, unchangeable part of Your very being]". (Psalm 89:8)

When I went through the fire that came to purify me, I did not burn; and when the floods of life came upon me, I did not drown, because God is faithful and true to His word.

God is _Love_

"Beloved, let us [unselfishly] love and seek the best for one another, for love is of God; and everyone who loves [others] is born of God and knows God [through personal experience]. He who does not love has not become acquainted with God [does not and never did know Him], for God is love. [He is the originator of love, and it is an enduring attribute of His nature]. By this the love of God was displayed in us, in that God has sent His [One and] only begotten Son [the One who is truly unique, the only

"One of His kind] into the world so that we might live through Him. In this is love, not that we loved God, but that He loved us and sent His Son to be the propitiation [this is, the atoning sacrifice, and the satisfying offering] for our sins [fulfilling God's requirement for justice against sin and placating His wrath]. Beloved, if God so loved us [in this incredible way], we also ought to love one another." (I John 4:7-10)

God is *Righteous*

"The law of the Lord is perfect [flawless]. Restoring and refreshing the soul; the statues of the Lord are reliable and trustworthy, making wise the simple.

"The precepts of the Lord are right, bringing joy to the heart; the commandment of the Lord is pure, enlightening the eyes.

"The fear of the Lord is clean, enduring forever; the judgments of the Lord are true, they are righteous altogether." (Psalm 19:7-9)

God is _Holy_

"There is no one holy like the Lord, There is no one besides You, there is no Rock like our God." (I Samuel 2:2)

"There is a river whose streams make glad the city of God, the Holy dwelling place of the Most High." (Psalm 46:4)

"Your way, O God, is holy [far from sin and guilt], what God is great like our God?" (Psalm 77:13)

"Exalt the Lord our God and worship at His footstool! Holy is He!" (Psalm 99:5)

"He has sent redemption to His people; He has ordained His covenant forever; Holy and awesome is His name – [inspiring reverence and godly fear]. (Psalm 111:9)

God is *Merciful*

"But God, being [so very] rich in mercy, because of His great and wonderful love with which He loved us…" (Ephesians 2:4)

"Blessed [content, sheltered by God's promises] are the merciful, for they will receive mercy." (Matthew 5:7)

"Therefore let us [with privilege] approach the throne of grace [that is, the throne of God's gracious favor] with confidence and without fear, so that we may receive mercy [for our failures] and find [His amazing] grace to help in time of need [an appropriate blessing, coming just at the right moment]." (Hebrews 4:16)

Chapter 6

<u>Character Faith</u>

Faith is one of my most favorite topics.

Having Faith in God shows your Character.

The World was formed through Faith.

Everything that exist in the world first

appeared in the mind of the inventor, who

believes that it is possible.

"But without faith it is impossible to

[walk with God and] please Him, for

whoever comes [near] to God must

[necessarily] believe that God exists and that He rewards those who earnestly and diligently seek Him." (Hebrews 11:6)

Rahab, showed her Faith in God when she hid the spies who came to spy out the land. "…only Rahab the prostitute and all [the People] who are with her in her house shall be [allowed to] live, because she hid and protected the messengers [scouts] whom we sent" (Joshua 6:17)

"Rahab was justified by works of faith, because she protected the spies and sent them away by a different route." (James 2:25)

Joshua and Caleb showed faith because they brought back a good report after spying out the promise land. Even though they saw the giants in the land, they choose to believe. They said, we are well able to take the land, let us go up at once.

"For just as the [human] body without the spirit is dead, so faith without works [of obedience] is also dead." (James 2:26)

Let your Character Light Shine!

As spiritual darkness increases upon the earth, the value of life has become of little importance.

Newspaper headlines are filled with reported killings of innocent men, women, boys and girls.

"...[Satan] has blinded the minds of the unbelieving to prevent them from seeing the illuminating light of the gospel of the glory of Christ, who is the image of God." (2 Corinthians 4:4)

Humanity is in need of salvation

through Jesus Christ. He is

the way, the truth, and the life. (John 14:6)

Jesus said, "I am the light of the world.

He who follows Me will not walk in

the darkness, but will have the light of

life." (John 8:12)

"I have come as light into the

world, so everyone who believes and

trusts in Me [as Savior-all those who

anchor their hope in Me and rely on the

truth of My message] will not continue

to live in darkness." (John 12:46)

You and I are the light of the world. As Disciples of Jesus Christ, your Character is the fruit that you are known by.

"You are the light of [Christ to] the world. A city set on a hill cannot be hidden; nor does anyone light a lamp and put it under a basket, but on a lampstand, and it gives light to all who are in the house. Let your light shine before men in such a way that they may see your good deeds and moral excellence, and [recognize and

honor and] glorify your Father who is

in heaven." (Matthew 5:14-16)

Light up the world with Character!

About the Author

Bonnie Leonard is the founder of **Women of Character Seminars**. She is a gifted Administrator, Motivator, and Teacher of faith-based and secular principles and disciplines that shape and develop Character foundations for success in all areas of life.

She possesses the ability to inspire, motivate, and empower; and is a dynamic speaker.

She holds a MBA from the University of New Haven; and a Bachelor degree in Business Studies from Quinnipiac University.

Bonnie draws from her education, training and personal relationship with the Lord Jesus Christ and believes that she has a mandate to bring women to their next level of success.

Contact Info: P.O. 672, Marion, CT 06444
www.womenofcharacterseminars.com